What people say about...

WORKING WITH ALZ

"We are not an average dental practice and we do what is necessary to set ourselves apart in the mind of our patients. Alzay's methods are in sync with our approach and we support his mission of using non-conventional methods to build more "coveted" companies in the marketplace. I appreciate the work he does at Coveted Consultant and I am already considering working with him again for some of my upcoming larger projects."

Dr. Louis Kaufman DDS MBA, Kaufman and Kaufman Smile Design Studio, LLC

"Alzay's core competency is telling people how to do it right."

Maurice Cooper, Vice President, Holiday Inn, Americas at InterContinental Hotels Group

"Working with Alzay pushes you into your excellence. He leaves you no other choice, no outs and no shortcuts. In the end, you will be glad he did."

C. Nzingha Smith, Author at CN Smith Books

"One conversation with Alzay will provide more clarity than you may have thought you would get in any call. That alone makes the decision to work with him in any way easier. Every entrepreneur needs assistance on their path and I can only say that Alzay is someone I'm willing to have assisting me on my path. Clear, concise, action steps that you can put to use right away to help you achieve your money goals."

>   **Ingrid Geronimo**, President & Founder, Dancing
>   Dragonflies Wisdom, LLC

"I really appreciate our Coveted Consulting session. In 30 minutes you unlocked my frustration and charted out steps for immediate success. I received achievable action steps and an unintimidating timeline for expansion and growth. Thanks."

>   **Amin Aleem**, CEO, Cornerstone Accounting

"Alzay is the real deal. He listens to you, asks you questions and makes sure you don't go off track. His product launch techniques are simple to learn, easy to implement and above all, they work! I learned a lot, especially the importance of giving value to your clients, and that has made all the difference."

>   **Marjan Glavac**, CEO, The Busy Educator

YOU ROCK! Thanks a million! I feel like singing "I can see clearly now the rain is gone…I can see all the obstacles in my way…." LOL

    Ra'Shaunda Fuller CEO at Social Butterfli Media Group

"Thank you so much for tailoring the product launch ideas to my specific needs and niche. You gave me an easy to follow guideline to get me started, one that I could use immediately. No matter where you are in the process, Alzay can take your product launch to the next level."

    Tricia Browne, Creator, Handmade Body Care

"Alzay asks deep, probing questions which get to the heart of any business challenge. He is then able to quickly assess the situation and offer sound, strategic advice. Alzay really cares about his clients, and he is committed to their success. He is also generous with his time, talent, and resources!"

    Ford Myers Career Coach and Author at Career Potential

"In regards to hiring Alzay, I definitely saw the return on my investment."

    Dr. Tiffany Bussey, Morehouse College, Director Entrepreneurship Center

"It is a pleasure for me to comment on the excellent work that Alzay Calhoun did for our healthcare practice. His knowledge of our industry and passion for success is immeasurable. He is exceptionally capable and personable individual, and I have great respect for his high-quality work, and his responsible and trustworthy character. Mr Calhoun thoroughly understands the portfolio of ad products available for him to sell, and is able to develop solutions for potential advertisers that fulfill individual needs.

He understands that importance of the customers and how they enable us to thrive as a business. Mr. Calhoun has shown a willingness to go beyond, and provide the most complete and thorough work not only in a timely manner, but also well-ahead of his estimated timeline for completion of the project. He is ALWAYS in contact with his customers and does not compromise his integrity. It is my privilege to recommend Mr. Alzay Calhoun, Owner of Coveted Consultant marketing firm."

Dr. Timothy Kimball, President/CEO, Texas Psychological and   Consultation Services

"I would like to thank you for reaching out to provide marketing assistance to my small accounting practice. You provided exactly the services you stated in a very swift manner. I would not have been able to put my company's name out in front of as many people without your help. Thank you for providing the spark that will push my business to the next level.

> **Carl D. Long**, Owner, CDL Accounting and Tax Services

"Alzay, with Coveted Consultant was able to, in a very short period of time, put together a radio commercial for my business, and help raise our exposure level tremendously! He was able to do this with almost no knowledge of who we are or what we do. This is truly incredible.

After this, he did a follow up interview that identified where the strengths and weaknesses of my business lay, and offered some very insightful suggestions as to how to make improvements. He broke it up into very manageable chunks and set me up with a plan that will allow me to grow faster and more effectively than would have been possible in the current state of affairs.

I will definitely be working with him in the future, and I would recommend you do as well."

> **Kyle Lindsey**, President/CEO, Kyle Lindsey Custom Homes, LLC

Answers:

17 Strategies For Building a One-of-A-Kind Consulting Practice

by Alzay Calhoun

DEDICATION

This book is dedicated to YOU, the well trained, deeply experienced expert who aspires to create the most impactful consulting business your industry has ever seen.

I have written this book with you in mind. The books is based off the most frequently asked questions I get in conversation with my clients. I have tried to answer each question succinctly and provide next steps (where appropriate).

Even if you do not find your immediate answer this book should help cut through the clutter to help you focus on the right question. The truth is, clarity comes in pieces and I trust that this book plays a role in the clarity you seek.

Onward.

CONTENTS

CHAPTER 1
WHAT ARE SOME EXAMPLES OF COVETED POSITIONING?

We are going to talk about three examples of coveted positioning outside the world of consulting. We are going to step outside of the advice and service based business and to look at some business models from very established companies in order to appreciate what coveted looks like.

Disney World. Disney World knows what their "WOW" looks like. If you are going to be coveted and be special in the eyes of your clients then you have to deliver on "WOW". You cannot do that if you don't know what "WOW" looks like. Not only does Disney understand their best experience, but they are also fully committed to it across the park.

Wherever you go, every employee has bought into delivering a "WOW" experience for you. The park is called the Happiest Place on Earth and they earn that title to the very best of their ability. What is very important to mention is that Disney World lives up to that "WOW" long after their founder Walt Disney has passed away. We know that coveted positioning and coveted thinking is engraved into this business because it lives way beyond the founder.

Starbucks. I can make this very plain by saying the following: Demi, Short, Tall, Grande, Venti and Trenta. If you know what those things are, you are a Starbucks customer. If you don't know what those things are, then you are not a Starbucks customer. They are all sizes of coffee. You can't walk into Starbucks and say you want a small, medium or large. They don't have it. They have very specific sizes and precise names for each size. What does that mean in regards to being coveted? Their customer speaks the same language they do. They've created a very specific language just for the size of cups they have and their customers share that language.

In your own business you should establish a language with your clients unique to your relationship. That's part of what makes you special and coveted. You literally speak a special language and that creates a special bond between you and your clients.

McDonald's. How does McDonald's help us think about coveted positioning? Everywhere you go, McDonald's serves the same thing, looks the same way and follows the same operation manual. They are the ultimate model of consistency and that consistency is the same worldwide. Anywhere you go in the world, McDonald's looks like McDonald's. The have completely invested in delivering a consistent offering in each and every location.

In regards to being coveted, they are the gold standard for a "fast food" restaurant. When we think about fast food, we think about McDonald's. They are the premier example of what it means to be a quick serve, fast food restaurant. All of their competition looks at them to be the leader and tell them where the industry and marketplace is going. They view McDonald's as the leader and if we're talking about coveted positioning, being seen as a leader in the industry is certainly part of being coveted.

The point here is that we can use examples way outside of our primary business to appreciate what it means to be coveted because the fundamentals are the same everywhere. Your job as the leader of your consulting firm is to commit to the same fundamentals that lead to coveted positioning.

CHAPTER 2
WHAT'S THE DIFFERENCE BETWEEN MY BUSINESS AND A COVETED ONE?

We are going to talk about what you really want from your consulting business. It is going to be great because we are going to skip the fluff and get straight to the point. We are going to talk about what you really want to do, what it is that you actually do, what coveted consultants do, as well as accept a new mentality that will deliver more value to your clients and your business.

What do you really want? The first thing you want is to be respected. You want people to appreciate you for what it is you do. The second thing is you want is to charge high fees. You don't want to be seen as a typical consultant in your industry. You want to be seen as someone special, as someone who demands extra attention and extra compensation. Third, you want time leverage. You don't want to be intimately involved with every single client. You want to be able to live a certain lifestyle and in order to do that you need certain leverage in your business. In summary, you want to be coveted. You want to be seen as specialized, high value consultant in your field. You want your client to see you above and beyond any possible competition because you do something excellent in their world.

What YOU do. First, you are working too hard for each

of your clients. Somewhere down the line you bought into the idea that the harder you work, the more that client will value you. You know that's not true, but you keep doing it anyway. Second, you strive to know everything. Somewhere along the way someone told you that you need to know all that there is to know about your expertise. So you keep reading, researching, interviewing and traveling, trying to "know everything". It doesn't appear that client cares... no matter how much you know. Third, you believe that all work is good work. Since you committed to the responsibility of "putting bread on the table", you feel forced to accept every job that comes down the pike because "all money is good money".

What THEY do. What are the coveted consultants doing in their business? They are practicing client selection. They aren't working hard for every client. They specifically choose what clients they want to work with, not work for. Coveted consultants focus on value. They don't care what they charge; the money doesn't mean anything to them. It's a matter of value. What should your business focus on to move your client the furthest, the fastest? That is how value is defined and that is what clients pay to experience.

Additionally, coveted consultants know what is valuable and they create that success over and over. If you are consistently producing a high level service that clients value, then you can't be anything but coveted. You can't be anything but special. Being phenomenal every single time is absolutely special. What do you need to do to make that transition right now?

Accept a NEW mentality. Clients do not choose you because you work hard, clients choose you because you consistently deliver high value services. That means that your job is not to work hard, your job is not to always be available. Your job is to figure out what your highest value service is and then figure out how to consistently deliver it over and over and over.

As of today you have a new job and that new job is going to create more value in the lives of your clients. As a result, you will experience much more value in your business. Use the information in this article to breathe new life into your business and that of your clients.

CHAPTER 3
HOW CAN I BECOME A COVETED CONSULTANT?

We are going to talk about how to become a coveted consultant. We are going to think about it in three steps, which will get you well on your way of becoming the leader of your consulting business, instead of being the consulting business. Once you separate yourself from the business by creating systems for your business, you can then focus on developing yourself and your business.

Separate you from the business. You know too much about your business. You know everything about your business. You know the history of your business. You know the future of your business. You know all the clients. You know how to do every single step of client service. You know how to do all the client follow-up. You know the bookkeeping and accounting. You know all the web design, work and edits that were done. You know way too much about your business and because you know too much, you end up doing too much.

Because you know how to invoice your clients, you just

do it. Because you know the answer to that question, you just answer it. Because you know how to do web design work, you just do it. Because you know too much and you do too much, you don't see nearly enough of your business.

You don't have the perspective of all that is going on because you can't step away from the work long enough to really see how all the pieces fit together. You also don't see how inefficient you are, because you're always busy. In other words, you aren't really running a business, you are the business.

Systemize your business. This step deals with the transition of going from you being the business, to you running the business. What are typical results for clients? When a client works with you and your company, what do they typically end up with? What is the typical end result? Secondly, what are clients guaranteed to experience? This is not necessarily what they get or what they become at the end of working with you, but what happens to them along the way. What are the four, five or six things that they are guaranteed to experience while they work with you. Have you clarified that. Thirdly, will any of those things happen if you aren't around? You know what the typical result is and what the clients normally experience when they're working with your company.

If you're not standing there watching everything, directing all that traffic every day, do those things happen? If your answer is not to that, then you have some systems to build because your clients need to experience a high level result from you and your company without you having to direct every single piece of every single activity. You need some systems in place to ensure that the typical results can happen and that the classical experience of working with you is always true and always valuable.

Develop yourself. This is the third major step you need to do. Once you have separated yourself from the business and you've put some systems around your business, then you can think more about you as the leader of that business. You have to answer questions such as:

What do you need to know? There are some things that you know now, that you really shouldn't know, but there are some things that you really need to know about your business and where it is going in the future.

Who do you need to meet? Are there new promotional partners that you need to meet? Is there a new mentor that you need to interact with? Are there new employees that you need to pursue and invite them to your company?

How do you refuel? This is very important in regards to how you develop yourself. How do you stay excited about your own business? How do you stay sharp, in tune and excited about what you do? How do you identify those things? Are those things a part of your daily interactions or part of your monthly or quarterly to-do list? Are they a part of what you do as you lead your business. If you are not excited about your business, then you won't create an exciting business. Your clients won't want to get involved with an unexciting business. In other words, until you become better, sharper, faster at being a leader of your company, then you can't produce a coveted consultancy.

Notice that today we did not talk about how to be a better consultant, because that's not your problem; you are a fine consultant. You need to get better at the business of consulting and that is your challenge today.

CHAPTER 4
WHAT IS MISSING FROM MY BUSINESS PLAN?

We are going to talk about creating a business plan for a consultant and I'm going to take a specifically different approach than most. Most times when we talk about a business plan, we talk about target market, finance needs, internal structure, and service offerings.

Those things are important and they have a place. In most business plan outlines I see, a very important thing is missing. What is missing in the plan is a mention of your importance as the creator of this business. You are the primary visionary who has taken responsibility for crafting what this business is going to be. What plan do you have in place to ensure your role as leader is never interrupted or distracted? This article will help explain your new role so you can understand how important it is to the health of your future business planning.

Dreaming is now a part of your job. In other words, this means you always have to know what your company's Big Picture is. Where is your business now, where is it headed, what is in between point A and point B? How do you plan execute on this dream? You must have a way to get from point A to point B. You may call it a method, process or philosophy. In any case, you are responsible for explaining how your company will finally reach the Big Picture. Who will help you along the way? You know you must have a team. What kind of help do you need to bring your Big Picture to life? These are the new questions you must respond to every day.

Your ability to dream is attacked every day. You have to appreciate the fact that your dream is going to get attacked each and every day. For example, there are going to be clients that say "No" to you and every time you hear "No" fear will creep in and make you a little more nervous for the next time. Nervousness makes your dream feel a little less realistic. Nervousness is a dream attacker. You can't be afraid of clients that say "No". If you have a dream and you've got a Big Picture, then it's worth pursuing.

You also have to be careful of disagreeing experts. There will always be someone who disagrees with you. Some of those people will have more credentials, longer titles behind their name, more experience, and more clients. It doesn't matter. If you have a legitimate and realistic Big Picture, it's worth pursuing and you can't let disagreeing experts talk you out of what you know is a great opportunity for you and your potential clients.

Lastly, you have to look out for personal fatigue. If you build a business that is based around your energy, sooner or later you will get tired and make poor decisions based on fatigue. You have to look out for personal fatigue so that doesn't become an active attack on your Big Picture.

How do you plan to protect the dream? First, you protect it with processes. There is a unique way you go about doing things and you need to clearly communicate your methods to all of your stakeholders. Your clarity is important so you can explain, articulate, and train people on your company's specific methods. Everyone needs to understand that the methods are important because they ensure consistent excellence.

In that same light, documentation is very important. When you do something well and deliver at a high level, you need to write it down. Write down your process, time to completion, and your expectations for the team member who will do the task over from you. Finally here is another reminder about the importance of team. You need people in your environment who understand your Big Picture and are willing to defend it with their effort. They are willing to work hard to bring it to life and cut out those things that don't fit.

There are a lot of business plan methodologies, examples, templates and formulas out there. You need to make sure that the business plan you create protects you, the Big Picture, and the big dream that you're putting forward. If the big dream dies, your business will die.

CHAPTER 5
WHAT MUST I HAVE IN MY BUSINESS PLAN?

The topic of of this chapter is how to create a business plan for a business consulting business. You are a professional, you've worked in your field for a number of years, and now you're prepared to offer your specific expertise to other businesses. What should you focus on as you plan out your new business? My suggestion is to focus on a successful client attraction model.

What problem will you solve? Every business has its own unique set of problems, but there are some things that are consistent in almost every business. Here are some short examples: lead generation, customer service, management consulting, legal structure, social media, public relations, and salesmanship. These are just some of the issues you could consult on as a business consultant. What you have to do is be clear about which problem you are solving. Be careful, do not focus on the service you are offering. Instead, focus on the specific problem your client has in their business. What words are they using to define their problem and what solution are you prepared to offer that matches their problem as they describe it?

How will you reach them, consistently? There are a number of ways to market or promote a business. You can do it through networking, referrals, live events, and direct mail just to name a few. Here is the part you have to focus on, you have to be clear and confident that you can use your resources, your advantages, and your strengths create a strategy to find your best client over and over again. Be careful of the silver bullet dynamic where certain strategies seem impactful, but require resources that your business doesn't have. Focus on what you have access to, what you understand, and what you know how to do and use those methods to consistently attract your best client.

Make a decision! You have to commit to trying your chosen strategy until it works. You have to know that when you use a certain strategy, you're going to get a certain response. You have to work the strategy until you really understand what that response is. To that end, regard all information as feedback. It doesn't matter whether you like your feedback or not, all information helps you make smarter business decisions. You have to be consistent with your strategy in order to clearly understand the quality of the feedback you are getting in response. Respond to your feedback by revising the plan accordingly. Whether you choose to try the plan again with no changes or you choose make specific tweaks, you have to revise the plan as you go. The plan is not a static document that lasts forever. Just because you've written something down, it doesn't mean the world is going to respond exactly how you intended. You have to make some adjustments to stay relevant in your marketplace.

There are a lot of ways to craft a business plan, but there are some things that need your immediate attention. One of those urgent things is your client attraction strategy. You have to know what service you are offering, what problem it solves, who you plan to reach, how you plan to reach them, and commit to refining your process over time. This is a core fundamental that must be included in your business consulting business plan.

CHAPTER 6
WHY IS IT SO HARD TO FIND GREAT CLIENTS?

We are going to talk about how to start a consulting business and I'm going to use the analogy of shopping for formal wear. You shop for a new clients the same way you shop for a new dress or a new suit. The first time you go shopping, you're probably not going to find the exact clients you want. You need to go through a process of learning how to find the exact client that fits your business the best way. This article will explain that process.

Best case scenario: You find a boutique. You find a small, specialized store that is just for you; a store that specializes in your style, your size and your body type. If you could make a store that was tailor made for you, walking into the store would reveal every suit, tie, pair of shoes, or dress you needed. It is the same principle with your clients. The best scenario is to find one particular place to find every client you would ever need. It would be a tailor made solution for your business. It is the best case scenario and your ultimate end goal. However most companies have a different reality, especially in the beginning, and it looks more like a worst case scenario.

Worst case scenario: You visit a shopping mall. When you visit a shopping mall there are all kinds of options, probably too many options. In a shopping mall exploration is mandatory. You're going to have to walk the entire mall to see all of what's inside and then mix and match items from different stores. For the men: you may have to get your suit from the first store, shirt from the second store and tie from the third store. For the ladies: you may have to get your heels from the first store, dress from a second store and purse from a third store. This is the process of shopping and you have to figure things out. In that process of going to the mall, you begin to learn more about your style and which stores carry the best looks for you. The next time you shop your experience will be more directed and efficient. In your business you have to be willing to shop around and find the types of clients that are the best fit you. Along the way, you will learn more about your style and where your best clients are. Each time you go shopping for clients your experience will be more directed and efficient.

How to find clients that "fit" you. In the process of finding formal wear that fits you, it may be necessary to window shop. You may not have to walk into every store, but you may have to walk in front of many different stores, see what they have on display, and consider if you want to explore the store further. You may have to take notes as you walk from store to store to remember what makes one store different from another. You may also have to take pictures, because sometimes your written word will not provide a good enough description. Lastly, you are going to have to review your research. You are going to have to go back to your desk, look at your notes and then prioritize what makes the most sense for you and your business. Shopping for clients is the same. There are many places you could spend your time, energy, and money. You have to assess all reasonable options and make the best decision you can.

The important thing in any consulting business is having clients, but you have to appreciate the fact that finding the best client is a process. It doesn't happen automatically; you have to have some patience. It's much like shopping for the perfect suit or the perfect dress.

CHAPTER 7
AM I SABOTAGING MY OWN BUSINESS?

We are going to talk about phantom problems. These are problems you believe exist, but don't. I get this a lot from my clients and you may have a similar issue. You believe you have a specific understanding of the challenge your business faces and you want an answer... now. You want a silver bullet o r magic solution that immediately resolves it. If this sounds familiar, let me suggest that what you believe is the problem isn't the problem at all. Some common examples will help explain what I mean.

I need a better time management solution. You are looking for a calendaring system, list management system, appointment scheduling system, a new app or a new website that will help manage your behavior or time management. The truth is, this is not really what you need.

It's not about time management... it's about priorities. Certain things are more important than other things. For example, how important is breathing to you? What is more important to you than breathing? Well then, by definition everything else is second to breathing. Additionally, how important is eating to you? If breathing is first and eating is second, then all the business tasks are third. If we keep thinking this way and take a look at your consulting business, certain tasks are as important as breathing and eating. That means every other task must come after these.

Once you set your priorities, it's easier to figure out where your time should be spent.

It's not about time management... it's about clarity. You have to be clear about what is important to your business and what isn't. That means you have to separate your thoughts, ideas and strategies; look at them individually and figure out which are most important and mean the most to your business. Ask yourself, "Do I truly understand each element of the problem?" If you are not clear on what the issue is, you are doomed to solving the wrong problem over and over.

It's not about time management... it's about panic. You create to-do lists that are so long they intimidate you. You see how much you have to do and it creates panic, anxiety, and stress. You have to flip that. You must be able to look at your to-do list and not be intimidated by its length or what's on it. As you develop the discipline to look at your tasks in a different way, the scary and uncomfortable emotions will subside.

I need cash, now! The second major point that my clients come to me with quite often is "I need cash, now! I need customers, now! I need money!" I suggest to you that it's not about the money. For example, what will you do between today and the day when the money arrives?

Whatever you do, it has to be something healthy. How do you know your new money is going be spent any differently than your previous money? If you know you made a mistake in the past, how do you make better decisions moving forward? You have to think hard about it. Also, how much money do you really need? How many clients and engagements do you really need? Until you are clear about your need, any new money that comes in the business is likely to be spent just as poorly as the old money.

I can't trust my employees. Another common discussion I get from my clients is, "My employees don't do good work. This is a very limited belief about your current employees. You may say, "John Brown is a jerk and nobody likes him." That may be true, but what is also true is that you hired him! Maybe it is time to let him go. If John Brown is that unhealthy to the environment, he doesn't belong. The same is true for known underperformers. You need to let them go if you can't train them to be better. The point is, don't let your business be subject to a mistake that was made from a hiring perspective. You can fix it!

The real issue is your perspective on the problem. You don't have an issue with your time, money, or employees. It's your perspective on these things that has you intimidated. For example, you may be too close to the issue. When you stand too close to an issue you are able to see all the minor details, but you can't get a wide enough perspective make major business decisions. Talk to an expert, consultant, or coach to provide some feedback and be a mirror to you. When you fully embrace the appropriate perspective you can prioritize the issues that really deserve your attention.

These are all examples of phantom problems. These are problems you believe exist, but don't. If you as a leader can achieve a different perspective on your own company, you can solve problems more quickly. Push for a clear perspective on the root cause and commit to the behaviors that will resolve the issue. Think hard today about what it is that's keeping your company from growing. Think about what that real problem is, get help if you need it, and grow your business, like you should.

CHAPTER 8
WHAT'S WRONG WITH MY TO-DO LIST?

We are going to talk about how overwhelm kills your consulting business. Overwhelm is an emotion and like all emotions it has a trigger that causes it to happen. Check to see if you have these tell-tale signs that may be causing you to feel overwhelmed. Look at the suggestions on how to deal with feeling overwhelmed and how you can turn the situation around in order to add maximum value to your life and your business.

Overwhelm is an emotion, not a business problem. Feeling overwhelmed is the same as feeling happy, sad, encouraged, disappointed, excited, or angry. Emotions are a response to something. You have to address the event that triggers their intensity. What trigger event do you notice? Can you point out what is happening in your business that is making you feel overwhelmed?

To-do lists are a trick. To-do lists are a major culprit of feeling overwhelmed. Do you have things on your to-do list that never move? Do you have things listed to help you avoid the real work of your business? If you have an unfocused to-do list, it only stresses you out. Yes, you will be busy, but the tasks don't move your business forward. Actually, this unfocused to-do list only adds to the frazzled and unfocused felling that leads to feeling overwhelmed.

Do things that matter. In order to get things back in focus, do things that matter.

Commit to you. Commit to the things you know you need to do so that each day builds on the one before. Commit to the things that improve your expertise, your understanding of the daily business operations, and your understanding of your clients. Do the things that make you a better leader of your consulting firm.

Commit to your business. What are the things that must be prioritized in order to improve your business and help it produce a better outcome for your clients? Does your sales process need refining? Should you re-commit to your client retention strategy? Does your service offering need to be improved? Recommit to those things.

Commit to your employees. Recommit to your employees. There are things you owe to your employees, clients, vendors and outsourcers. These groups support you directly and indirectly. Make sure you are providing for them in the very best way you can.

Be honest. Be honest in your assessment of you and your business. It may be something in the above list or something else. Only you know exactly what it is. Whatever the issue, go after the things that actually matter to the growth of your business.

Solve the time management trick. In order to solve the time management trick, you need more than a time management hack. You need more systems in place, more procedures, and deliberate ways of producing high level results. More systems also means that you need less stuff. You don't need more software, more employees, more sheets of paper, or more templates.

Additionally, you have to be able to measure success. What does success actually mean? You have to be able to differentiate between a good result, a great result, and a poor result. Your environment, your team, your vendors, and your employees also have to be able to know the difference between a good, a bad and a great result.

Finally, in order to better manage your time you must prioritize. Choose the things that are most important to you and make sure those things happen. If you are consistently doing the things that matter most and those are highest on the priority list, then you'll do them well. You will end up getting more momentum in your business simply because you can provide the best energy on the things that provide the best value. While it makes simple sense, it is easier said than done. It requires heavy commitment.

CHAPTER 9
WHY DOES IT FEEL LIKE SOMEONE ELSE IS
RUNNING MY BUSINESS?

Let's talk about the invisible systems that run your business. Every business is composed of systems to ensure things get done. These systems can be created consciously or unconsciously. The most dangerous systems are created unconsciously. Since you don't know they exist, you don't know if they help or hurt. In your own consulting business you need to take the time to be aware of how work is done every day. Use this article to pinpoint what systems are helping or hurting.

Do you believe in systems? Some consultants believe that systems are everything and you should have them in place in order to avoid failure. Other consultants believe that systems stifle creativity and should be avoided at all cost. My argument on this matter is that not only are systems important to your business, but you also have invisible systems in place that threaten the success of your business.

Invisible systems are a silent threat. Whether you realize it or not and whether you believe it or not, there are invisible systems at work. You have processes, methods, and procedures that help you get work accomplished. Do you see all of your systems? Do you understand all of your systems? There are predictable systems that are present in your everyday business, regardless of whether you understand them or not. Here are some checks to see if invisible systems are present in your business.

Checking your business for invisible systems. In order to help you check your business for invisible systems, there are a few tell-tale signs you should consider:

You get the same result over and over. You know what your expectations are, but you get a sub-par result every time you try. Something you can't see might be affecting these results.

You don't know how a certain result is achieved. You may know that a specific person, software or equipment gives you a result in your business, but you don't exactly know how that works. It is best to understand what gives you the result and make that a visible system to you.

You only do a specific task when something breaks. You scramble to solve an issue when a customer makes a complaint, software breaks down, or an employee leaves. This happens because you didn't see the issue coming and you were going day-by-day, instead of working with a process. That occurrence has revealed an invisible system, which gives you the opportunity to take a look at it, understand it and improve it.

Developing better systems. Now that you understand

that there are invisible systems at work, we can focus on developing better systems by following a few simple steps:

1. Get a clear picture of what you want. Be clear with your team, clients and vendors so that everyone clearly understands your intended results.

2. Create metrics you can believe in. Now that you know what you want, be clear about the steps required to get to your desired end result.

3. Commit to a process. Make sure you see the process all the way through. It is important that you keep going, even it if doesn't work perfectly the first time.

4. Get help. This is a new situation, so it is important that you get any help you may need. You can ask your employees for feedback or hire a consultant to see if they can provide an outside perspective to pinpoint the invisible system and bring it to the surface.

CHAPTER 10
CAN I RUN MY BUSINESS WITHOUT REFERRALS?

We are going to talk about marketing for consultants and I am going to bust a myth that is commonly shared among consultants. The myth is: referrals are the lifeblood of a consultant's business. The philosophy continues by explaining if you are in the world of consulting and you want to build a consulting business, then you need to have a plethora of referrals. Today I am attacking that myth because it is not true and it steers a lot of consultants down the wrong path. Let me explain.

Referrals are great. First, the common understanding is that world of mouth is the best marketing and that is generally true because it's free. When people discuss your business in your absence, that's free promotion. That is a good deal. Second, it is often said that referrals create the best leads and that's also true. When people have been referred, typically they are already sold on doing business with you and you don't have to do any heavy selling. Third, common knowledge is referrals cut through the client's red tape. For example, if you are selling to an organization with two, three, or four decision makers being referred limits the amount of engagement you need to have with each and every person. There is already a sense of comfort with you and you can begin the your good work faster. All of those things I agree with, but there are a number of things not typically mentioned about referrals.

Referrals are flawed. You have to ask for referrals. Referral clients do not magically appear and past clients don't walk up to strangers and say "Hey, you should do business with John Brown." You must ask your existing client base to refer you. There has to be a process, a procedure or a method through which you consistently ask for referrals. Next, when someone gives you names of referrals there has to be a very structured way you respond and follow-up. This is a system and this system needs to be built and refined. Additionally, you need a group of existing clients if referrals are going to work for you. Who is going to refer you? Only those who have experienced your services already. So if you don't have an existing base of clients, you don't have anybody that can refer you. Finally, you can't control referrals. It is hard to consistently put your business on a growth path because you don't know when your next set of referrals are coming. If you don't know where your next influx of business is coming from it is difficult to plan, hire, and budget like a mature business.

Coveted Consultants know they must advertise. Advertising allows you to measure return on investment. If you spend $1,000 for an advertisement you can measure how many clients you earned as a result of that advertisement. Maybe for every $10,000 you spend you get three clients as a result. Maybe for every $2,750 you spend you get eight clients as a result. Whatever the return is, you can measure it. You don't need an existing client base, so you are not stuck if you don't have clients to refer you. In fact, you can advertise without any existing clients at all. Most importantly, advertising increases the level of control and predictability in your business. As you refine your process, you learn that if you spend a certain amount of money, you will receive a certain number of clients.

Coveted Consultants know that marketing strategy involves a mix of activities. There are a number of things your business will deploy at the same time. You will mix referrals, advertising, launch campaigns, phone selling, etc in order to develop an intelligent marketing mix. That is my challenge to you today. Don't just focus on referrals, but on your entire marketing mix, including advertising.

CHAPTER 11
WHERE CAN I FIND A NEW CLIENT...FAST?

We are going to talk about marketing for professional services. I am also going to put you on a path to getting your very next client right now. Let's get started.

Who are you? I am assuming you are a consulting company and you focus on one of the following things: accounting and financial services, management consulting services, technology services, marketing and communications or legal services.

What do you want? You want your expertise valued, your time leveraged and most certainly, more clients.

What should you avoid? You should avoid changing your business card, revising your website, managing your social media accounts, or reading any more industry publications. That is not where your problem is.

What else should you avoid? You should also avoid stressing over it, hoping it will fix itself, getting opinions from others, learning any new skills or pushing it to an employee.

What should you do RIGHT now? What would a coveted consultant do and what should you be doing at this very moment? First of all you should stop and think about how you got your last client. Write it down and then do the process again.

Quite often the first place consultants look for answers is outside of themselves and their organization, but it pays off to first clear your head and look for answers within.

CHAPTER 12
WHY DOES NO ONE UNDERSTAND WHAT I DO?

Let's talk about explaining your services in the best way possible, so your clients understand what you are trying to convey and get excited about it. The best way to go is to explain it to them as if you were talking to a five year old. You must keep in mind the distractions your client faces and work around them in order to get your point across. You must also understand when it is time to accept your client's decision and move on. Use this article to create a roadmap of how to best explain your services and products to your clients.

Client is distracted. Just like a five year old our client is distracted and has a lot of things going on. They have their own priorities before you showed up. They have other important things to take care of, besides talking to you. For this reason you have to make sure that you get their attention quickly. You will not have a lot of time to talk to your client, so be brief. You may have a full hour for your meeting, but you will only have their attention for the first few minutes. Make the most of those first few minutes. Be brief, be powerful, be strong and grab their attention quickly.

Simplify the concept. In much the same way as a five year old who has not learned big words yet, your client may not know the concepts you use in your everyday vocabulary. They may have heard them before, but they haven't mastered them. In order to keep things simple, save the fancy vocabulary and only communicate the essentials. Only tell them what they need to know in order to make an intelligent decision. Also, as you simplify the concept, tell them what the first couple of steps are and then tell them how the engagement will end. This way they clearly understand what they need to do to get started and what to expect from the relationship.

Remember the client has to make their own decision. Just like a five year old who doesn't want to go somewhere, the client can be a heavy weight. You cannot carry or manipulate them so you need them to make their own decision. Use the notes below to encourage your client to make a decision in their own best interest.

Don't force: Do not force your client to do anything that they don't want to do.

Don't beg: Do not beg them. If they don't see it in their best interest, don't oversell it.

Be careful of incentives: Whatever you promise a five year old, ice cream, fun times, etc you better keep that promise or you are going to have pain. It is the same way with your clients; whatever promise you make you better own up to that promise.

Don't whine: If they say "no", then the answer is no. If they say "yes", take the "yes" and keep moving. There is no need to whine and provide additional information on why things are the way they are. Your client doesn't care and that five year old doesn't care.

At some point... stop asking: There is a point in the conversation where you understand if that client has interest or not. Once you have a sense of that, stop talking. Even if there is more to say, that client or that five year old has already decided.

Five year olds will do anything that sounds fun. A five year old will do anything that sounds fun and your clients are the same way. If they know that interacting with you is going to be a pleasurable experience, it is easier for them to commit.

Be excited. Be exciting: When you communicate with your client be excited and be exciting. Actually have interest in what you are offering to them because you believe in it. Make that interaction with the client a pleasurable and fun experience.
Be benefit driven: Itemize the benefits and explain them all upfront. We want to make this into something your client or that five year old really wants to join in on.

Be straight forward: There is no need for long, flowery stories. If they get something, then tell them that they get it. If they don't get something, then tell them that they don't get it. The simpler the better.

Have fun without them: Make sure your client knows you are going to have fun with this experience separate from their choice to come with you or not. Your client needs to know you are not waiting on them.

This article is all about helping you better explain your services in a completely different way than most consultants. Break it down like you're talking to five year old. Remember what you have to do and how you have to behave in order to get a five year old excited. Treat your clients the same way. It's not about being condescending; it's just about being as real and as natural as you can. Clients will pick up on your sincerity the same way children do. Give them as much honest, natural, and wonderful energy as you can and see what happens when your clients respond.

CHAPTER 13
SO, I'M NOT SUPPOSED TO DO ALL OF THE WORK?

Let's talk about what your real job is when you're leading a consulting company. There are many hats you need to wear in order to keep your business moving forward, but you certainly don't have to wear all the hats within the company. There are tasks you should focus on in order to ensure the success of your business, while leaving other tasks to your employees. This article will help you focus on what your job is as a leader of your consulting business and what you should and should not be doing.

What your job isn't. Your job is not to be the face of the business. You don't have to put your name on every single product or on every single white paper or business card that goes out. You don't have to put your face on everything and that should not be your primary focus if you're the leader of the company. You also don't have to be the "know it all" expert. It isn't your job to know everything, not to mention it is extremely hard. If you put yourself in a situation where only you know and understand every single issue that your clients come across, you are setting yourself up for failure. There will be something that you don't know. Moreover, you don't have to be the core client romancer. You need clients, you have to interact with them and you need to be seen as their ally, but that is not only your job. Therefore, you don't have to attend all of their sessions, go to all of their networking events, attend every meeting and give every presentation. That is not your core responsibility. As you step back from these responsibilities, let me provide three other behaviors that are foundational if you're going to lead a consulting company the right way.

Recruit / Hire. You are responsible for recruiting and hiring. You have to make sure that you hire the right people who are attached to the right responsibilities. You have to assess someone for what they already bring to the table and match them with an appropriate job description. Second, you have to make sure you are putting quality inputs (people) in your systems so that you can get quality outputs (work) out of your systems. You have situations, processes, and systems in your business that are supposed to create a certain output. People need to come in to your organization, experience those systems, and then interact with clients at a high level. If you don't put in the right inputs, then you're going to end up with poor outputs. Third, you have to make sure you enjoy the people on your team. You must be sure they enjoy you and the culture you have prepared in your organization. If you don't enjoy them and they don't enjoy you, it doesn't matter how talented that person is. You cannot talk someone into a good relationship and a bad relationship doesn't fix itself later on. It is better to hire for attitude and train up their skills, than to hire for skill and try to convince them to improve their attitude.

Visionary. You have to be the core visionary and make sure that you, as the leader of the business, are always owning and articulating the big picture. There is a direction your business is going in, a certain client that you're trying to reach, and an experience you want that client to have. You have to own that big picture and explain it to everybody else in your organization. If you aren't focused on that, at some point the big picture loses clarity and your business loses potency. Second, you have to refine that big picture as new information comes. As you continue on the path of your big picture you will be introduced to new challenges like evolving competitors and changing client requirements. All of those things affect your big picture and you have to refine it as time goes on. Third, you have to catch new opportunities. New things come along and you have to be able to pounce on them. If your eyes aren't open for new opportunities you can't catch them, and if you can't catch them you don't experience new growth. Again, if you're not focused on your vision than all of these things pass you by.

Violently defend the culture of your organization. This might be the most important point of all. You must protect the sanctity of your environment.

Realize that there are threats to your environment: There are things that will otherwise interrupt your environment if you don't stop them. It could be competitors, bad internal attitudes, or wrong messages in the media. These are all threats and you have to work against them to keep your environment healthy.

Understand threats don't fix themselves: If you make a mistake and hire the wrong person in the company, it doesn't fix itself. You have to get in there and fix it, either by having one-on-ones to adjust their attitude or letting them go, if that's just the right course of action. Whatever the threat is, it will not fix itself and you have to directly address it.

No one is going to care like you: It is your company, your vision, and you gave birth to it. It's really important to you, but everyone else is going to care less than you. By definition it's not their baby, it's your baby. You have to make sure that you exhibit the highest level of caring for the overall business; it is a behavior they must see from you.

No one will see the threats like you will: No one is going to see the threats like you will and no one is going to be excited about eliminating them like you are. Again, you have to make sure that you exhibit the highest level of care and understanding about your business and you have to defend it, otherwise the threats will come in and take over.

If you're leading a consulting company, there's more to do than just being a friendly face on the business card. There are some behind the scenes responsibilities you must own because no one else can do them, but you.

CHAPTER 14
WHAT PERSPECTIVE SHOULD I HAVE AS THE LEADER OF MY BUSINESS?

How do you define your business leadership?

What are YOU going to do with your resources, skills, and experience? With all of your experiences I know you have a deep understanding of your market. The case studies, last minute projects, client meetings, inspirational bosses, challenging budgets, etc make for an excellent backdrop for your consulting company. But there is definitely something missing. What are YOU going to do with all of those resources? How do YOU define your business leadership?\

How will your skills create a unique legacy? When I say business leadership I'm not talking about an elevated title, large salary, and a cross functional team. I'm talking about having impact. I'm talking about making a difference. I'm talking about leaving a legacy. I'm talking about the kind of work you enjoy because you KNOW you are helping people. You can SEE the positive changes that are happening in the world around you.

What is your positive impact on people and organizations? And leadership does not require a million dollar budget or senior executive title. Business leadership is about having a positive impact on people and organizations. If you take the initiative to organize the cookout for the company picnic…that is leadership. If you create a customized seminar for the new trainees of your firm…that is leadership. If you managed the roll-out of a new, albeit small, product at your company..that is leadership.

Are you choosing your own path? The key is that YOU choose responsibilities that YOU find valuable and then EXECUTE them to the best of your ability. If the task matters to you, then it probably matters to someone else as well! Do not be afraid to put your skills on display. Do not be afraid to let people know what you are interested in. Your definition of business leadership is made clear by the positive impact you make on people and organizations.

CHAPTER 15
WHAT IS MY ROLE IN ATTRACTING NEW CLIENTS TO MY BUSINESS?

What are the crucial characteristics of effective leadership? Your competitors and predecessors provide excellent examples to study and learn from, but just because you are in business does NOT mean you automatically have an answer to this question. What you will soon see, if you haven't already, is that you have to answer this question for yourself. There isn't a "best way" to lead, and contrary to the many books written on the topic...no one can tell you how you should lead.

So then what should you do? First understand that leadership is much more of an art than it is a science. It isn't so much about what you do, but instead how you do it. The good news about this is you can use your own characteristics of effective leadership in almost any way you like. The bad news is this still leaves the question open to lots of interpretation. Here is some help to be sure you are most effective in your leadership role.

One of the main characteristics of effective leadership is clarity around the impact you want to make. If you are going to lead any group in any direction you must have your own picture of where you are going. Take the time to understand how your strengths will positively impact the situation you are in. Below are 6 simple questions to help you think through your leadership thoughts.

Who will benefit from your impact? Who are your major stakeholders? Are they defined by race, gender, or social status? Your impact has a target audience and you must know who they are.

What is your impact? What positive change is going to take place? Be specific on the difference you will make in the world of business.

When will your impact happen? How will you make the world a better place today? Don't "wait for the right opportunity". Instead, use your business savvy to affect positive change as quickly as possible.

Where will your impact occur? Is your focus local, regional, national, or global? Be clear about where your impact will occur and seek out the resources you need to enable it.

Why does this impact matter? Why should people prioritize your cause? How will you positively affect them? Make sure you can show people why they should be interested in the impact you are trying to make.

How are you going to deliver? What special skills do you bring to the table? Why should you be the one to lead the charge? Have confidence in your skills and show your competence daily.

Once you have clarity around the who, what, when, where, why, and how…execution is much easier. Now you can quickly explain to your team the direction you are taking them in. Your team will see the value of their efforts and this builds trust in the event challenges occur. This may seem simple, but give this a try and you will soon see why clarity is one of the most crucial and difficult characteristics of effective leadership.

CHAPTER 16
HOW CAN I KEEP CONTROL OF THE PEOPLE IN MY BUSINESS?

You can't.

Those who follow you (clients or employees) have a a choice on WHO they follow and WHY. Give your followers the right reasons.

For many, leadership is transactional. Someone gives instructions and someone else follows them. It's a matter of cause and effect. Step 1 then step 2. Simple and done.

However, YOU are much savvier than that. You realize that "giving instructions" is only one part of what happens when leaders lead. Let's talk about what else is happening...

What if I told you that people do what they CHOOSE to do. People choose to get up and go to work. People decide to send one email over another. People decide what to wear. People decide who they want to listen to and what response is most appropriate.

If this is true, that means that people choose to follow

your instruction. They listen to what you have to say, make a choice, and choose to follow/not follow. Even if they do exactly what you ask each and every time, they still made a choice to do so.

So then leadership isn't about what you tell your followers to do, it's about what your followers choose to do in response to what you say. Read that last sentence again, it may need a second time.

If you are still with me (and you still agree)…your leadership, guidance, and direction is about helping people make choices. Especially since you know they are going to make their own choice anyway.

Consider the viewpoint that your leadership is about helping people reach a decision that is good for both them and the environment they work in. This means that if people don't do what you ask they don't believe that what you asked works for them. They feel like something else is more important.

So ask yourself:
"What is most important to THEM?"
"Is what I ask of them in line with what THEY view to be important?"
"Do I truly value the fact that they will make their OWN decision no matter what I say?"

The magic here is to understand that your role as a leader is to influence people and not to decide for them. Deciding for them is impossible. They always have a choice.

CHAPTER 17
HOW WOULD I FIND A MENTOR FOR MY BUSINESS?

Finding a business mentor is an important part of growing and succeeding in your chosen career or endeavor. You need help. You need guidance. You need to speak with someone who has more experience than you. How do you find these people? What do you say when you encounter them? Use this article as a guide to locate your next business mentor.

Find common ground. This could be a school connection, hobby, passion, family origin or pet. It is much easier for someone to honor your request to speak with them when they feel like you have something in common with them. The more specific and personal connection the better. Since your mentor is going to be advising you on issues that are both personal and professional it just makes sense that you find sincere common ground that connects you.

Connect with honest intention. Do not be afraid to ask your prospective mentor for what you want. If you have a business and you'd like some feedback, then ask for feedback. If you believe that this prospective mentor can connect you with promotional partners who could help you, then ask for promotional help. If the prospective mentor asks has a network and you would like to be included, ask for an introduction. Whatever your intended goal is, ask in a professional straightforward manner.

Offer value to them. If you expect the prospective mentor to help you then you should be prepared to help them too. For example, you could share information about your common passions and interest. Whatever you have in common, open up a conversation and give them some of your deep insight. As another example, maybe it makes sense to offer a complimentary service. If your expertise can be of specific value to them feel free to offer it up as a way to honestly connect.

Ask for an appropriate next step. The last thing you need to do is to ask for the appropriate next step; whether it's inviting them to lunch, meeting them at their office, or setting up a phone meeting. There are a number of approaches, just be sure that your approach is easy from them to receive. You don't want to be a burden on their schedule. You want to make it easy for them to interact with you.

Finding a business mentor can be difficult without an appropriate approach. Use the steps found in this article to make a connection with someone you would like to mentor you.

ABOUT THE AUTHOR

"Alzay Calhoun is a highly sought after consultant and coach to businesses big and small. His passion is to permanently elevate the training standard for how to build a consulting practice. His strategies transform intelligent, technically oriented, stalled leaders of consulting firms into insightful, inspired, business architects. He wants to help you translate your expertise into an experience your clients can consume.

He typically charges $250 an hour for a telephone consultation. However he is passionate about helping experts thrive, and so he is extending a very limited opportunity for a complimentary 30-minute consultation to see if any or all of these strategies outlined in this book will apply to your business."

"If you would like to contact Alzay for a consultation, you must first call our Customer Hotline Number at 888-258-3534. This is a voice mail system and is never answered live. When prompted, please leave your name, business name, website url, and telephone number. This information will then be transcribed and sent to his assistant, who will review your request and contact you to schedule a time for the consultation."